# British Theatres and Music Halls

## John Earl

Published by Shire Publications Ltd,
Midland House, West Way, Botley, Oxford OX2 0PH, UK.
(Website: www.shirebooks.co.uk)

British Library Cataloguing in Publication Data:
Earl, John.
British theatres and music halls. – (Shire library; 442)
1. Theatres – Great Britain – History
2. Music-halls – Great Britain – History
I. Title 725.8'1'0941
ISBN-10: 0 7478 0627 6
ISBN-13: 978 0 74780 627 2

*Cover: Detail from an engraving entitled 'A London Music Hall' (unidentified), printed in
'Le Monde Illustré,' 1872.*
*Title page: Frank Matcham's 1910 façade for his London Palladium was a delightful elaboration of
the sober Corinthian Bazaar façade of 1868, which had also served as a front for Hengler's Circus.*

ACKNOWLEDGEMENTS
Thanks are due to Peter Longman, the Director, and my colleagues at The Theatres Trust, most
notably Fran Birch, whose collaboration at every stage was vital in producing a publishable work.
Ian Grundy's contribution was particularly important, especially when providing at short notice
excellent photographs of theatres otherwise unrepresented in the Trust's archives. Dr James
Fowler, Victor Glasstone, Rupert Rhymes and Michael Sell kindly read the manuscript in an early
version and made helpful suggestions, but any remaining errors, omissions or misplaced
emphases are mine alone.

Pictures were taken from the following sources; where necessary, they are lettered a, b, c, d
clockwise from top left: Ian Grundy, pages 9, 10b, 19b, 21a, 22c&d, 23a, 30a, 32, 36a, 38a, 41, 48a,
50b, 51a, 62; Alberto Arzoz (Axiom Photographic Agency), page 7; Fran Birch, pages 39b, 50a;
Critical Tortoise, page 13b; Hufton Crow, page 39a; Douglas Gaiety Theatre, pages 27b, 37b;
Hackney Empire (Nick Liseiko), page 57; Mike Hoban, page 52; Ralph Holt, page 22a; London
Metropolitan Archives, pages 47a, 48b; Ray Mander & Joe Mitchenson Theatre Collection, page 28;
Rob Moore, pages 20-21; John Muir, page 35a; National Monuments Record, English Heritage,
pages 42a, 44a, 46a; National Trust Photographic Library, page 12a; Northern Counties
Photographers, page 49b; Photogenics, page 10a; RCAHMS, page 19a; RHWL, page 36b; Rose
Theatre Trust, page 8; Savoy Theatre, page 43; Michael Sell, page 12b; John & Elizabeth Stanton
Collection, page 24; Steve Stephens, page 51b; Richard and Helen Leacroft Collection (David
Wilmore), page 46b; The Theatre Museum (Victoria & Albert Museum), page 31a; The Theatres
Trust (including the Faulkner Collection), pages 11b, 14b, 25, 30b, 34a, 40, 44b. The illustrations on
pages 1, 3, 4, 5, 6, 11a, 12c, 13a, 14a, 15, 16, 17, 18, 19c, 20a, 22b, 23b&c, 26, 27a, 29, 31b, 33, 34b, 35b,
37a, 42b, 44c, 47b, 54, 60 are from the author's collection.

Care has been taken to trace copyright holders but we apologise if any have been inadvertently
missed and will, if notified, rectify the omission in a future edition. JE.

Printed in China through Worldprint Ltd.

# Contents

*At the pantomime: a comfortably-off Victorian family in a box.*

# Introduction

Over the last five hundred years, theatre has been the one art in which Britain has consistently (if not quite continuously) led the world.

It still does. And yet there are distressingly few early buildings to represent Britain's glorious theatrical past. If you want to see a complete theatre built in Shakespeare's lifetime you must go to Vicenza, in Italy. Intact or nearly intact purpose-built theatres earlier than 1860 are extremely rare in Britain and we have only two whose present auditoria are earlier than 1800.

Eighteenth- and early-nineteenth-century theatres are quite numerous in mainland Europe (there are even one or two of the seventeenth century), some of them in thinly populated areas and infrequently used. So why have we so little to show for our unparalleled record of intense theatre activity?

The answer is simple. Theatres in Britain have rarely been designed as monuments of civic pride and, for most of the three hundred years following the Restoration, they never enjoyed royal, noble or even municipal patronage. Until relatively recent times all of our theatres have been built as unsubsidised commercial ventures. A theatre that failed financially was pulled down and the site sold. A theatre that made money was just as happily pulled down so that it could be replaced by a bigger and better one.

*Queuing for the cheap, unreserved pit benches in 1897. The presence of silk hats shows that the pit was not the exclusive preserve of the less privileged. Some inveterate theatre-goers made a point of attending the play for its own sake, rather than taking part in the social display of the boxes, stalls and dress circle.*

*A typical mid-Victorian theatre viewed from the stage. The 'out' signs were intended to show how safe the place was in case of fire. It was, in fact, a dangerous tinderbox that was fortunate in never having to put its escapes to the test.*

So much for numbers. A more general point about theatres also needs to be understood, and that is their unusual physical nature. A theatre auditorium of traditional form may be a richly decorated and furnished room but unlike, say, a ballroom or a great reception room, its design is intensely directional (everyone must be able to see the action) and it is always viewed in varying intensities of artificial light, never by daylight. It is also peculiar in that the great room seen by the public is commonly matched in volume by unseen backstage spaces.

*A backstage workshop at Drury Lane Theatre Royal making giant heads for the pantomime.*

*Under the stage in a Victorian pantomime house.*

# Theatres before 1800

The first theatre spaces within secular buildings took the form of temporary 'fit-ups'. Great halls like those in Hampton Court and the Inns of Court were regularly adapted for the purpose (Middle Temple Hall, for example, saw the earliest reliably recorded performance of Shakespeare's *Twelfth Night*), while barns and rooms in inns were fitted up in a simple manner for itinerant companies of actors. Galleried inn yards were even more readily pressed into service, setting a style which was given permanent form in the Elizabethan timber-framed open-air theatres.

These 'wooden O' playhouses in the fields of Shoreditch and Bankside were the first generation of substantial purpose-built public theatres since Roman times. They had a profound effect on the development of the drama and the shaping of the English language, but not a trace of them can now be seen above ground. The one important early theatrical relic that does remain is quite untypical. This is Inigo Jones's Whitehall

*The modern recreation of Shakespeare's Globe on Bankside, London.*

Banqueting House of 1618–22, designed to provide a suitable space for elaborately staged court masques.

The Commonwealth and Protectorate brought an end to theatre building and to most overt forms of performance between 1642 and 1660. At the Restoration of the monarchy the old, unroofed playhouses and a handful of private indoor theatres were abandoned, to be superseded by a new kind of theatre and a new style of staging, with changeable perspective scenery on the continental model.

Charles II granted patents to two theatre companies, creating in London a duopoly that was fiercely defended over nearly two hundred years against all attempts to present the drama elsewhere. These Carolean patents eventually settled on two sites, namely Drury Lane and Covent Garden. Patents of a more limited kind were later granted to a few other theatres (including the Haymarket) but the original grants became extremely valuable commodities, being divided into shares and passing from hand to hand.

Outside London, in the eighteenth century, royal patents were granted to a small number of theatres, which thus became Theatres Royal, but dramatic performance was otherwise regulated in a rather hit-and-miss manner by local magistrates, until their powers were clarified in 1788. This led to better security for the travelling companies of 'comedians' who, between the 1780s and the 1830s, built some hundreds of theatres in market towns. These companies each required a circuit of modest playhouses within a manageable geographical area of two or three counties. Circuit theatres (most of them were simply known as 'The Theatre') had to be closely similar in design and dimensions, so that 'stock' scenery could be transported to theatre after theatre and rehearsal times on nearly identical stages could be cut to a minimum.

These little theatres were open for limited seasons – Christmas, the assizes, race meeting weeks and so on – and at other times served as

*The remains of the Rose uncovered in 1989, the first physical evidence seen in modern times of an Elizabethan playhouse. The massive concrete blocks are twentieth-century piles that supported a building now demolished, but the outline of the theatre can be clearly seen in this relief image of the site by William Dudley.*

*The older of the two Georgian theatres in Bury St Edmunds, Suffolk, was a market hall, remodelled by Robert Adam in 1774. The exterior is unusually elegant for a theatre of the time, but the interior was stripped out after 1819.*

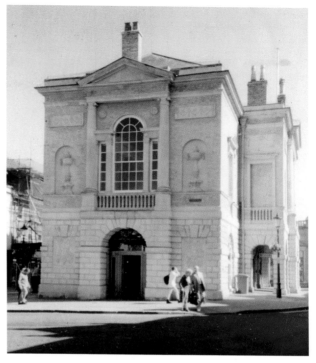

assembly rooms and ballrooms. Of this once numerous type a few remain recognisable, at least in outward appearance, today. Only one, in Richmond, Yorkshire, is complete and fully restored. It was built in 1788. Here alone, one can experience to the full the physical nature and unique atmosphere of a Georgian country playhouse.

Of the earliest Theatres Royal in the counties (they were usually the headquarters and maintenance centres of local circuits) there is only one relatively complete survival, namely Bristol Theatre Royal. This is also exceptional in having been founded as early as 1766, with alterations and embellishments in 1790 and 1800. Despite later alterations and extensions its auditorium is still recognisably Georgian and it is now Britain's earliest working theatre.

Robert Adam's Bury St Edmunds theatre of 1774, an architectural transformation of a 1734 market hall, now has no evidence internally of its theatrical life but it is an impressive landmark in the town. Bury St Edmunds is remarkable in having two Georgian theatres; the second falls into the next period.

*The Georgian theatre in Richmond, Yorkshire, 1788. This is the only completely restored survivor of the circuit theatres that once existed in their hundreds. Their deep forestages brought the actors into close contact with the audience.*

Below: *Bristol Theatre Royal, which was already more than twelve years old when it was granted a royal patent in 1778, is the oldest of the few active theatres in Britain with a recognisably Georgian auditorium.*

*Covent Garden Theatre Royal as rebuilt by Smirke in 1809. This theatre was destroyed by fire in 1856 and replaced by the present building by Edward Barry.*

# Changing times - 1800 to 1850

After 1800 the country circuits continued to flourish and two of Britain's most interesting early theatres date from this time. Cambridge Barnwell Theatre was built in 1814 by William Wilkins, a plasterer, to replace a portable theatre used at the fairs by the Norwich circuit. With its horseshoe-shaped tiers of boxes and upper gallery, the new theatre was a little more ambitious than the general run of barn-like playhouses, but still relatively unsophisticated. It was altered in 1926 by Terence Gray to become an historically significant open-stage theatre, the Festival. It is now a Buddhist temple.

*Cambridge Barnwell Theatre by William Wilkins the elder, 1814, was a Georgian theatre, converted to Britain's first end-stage in 1926 as the Festival Theatre. It has been a mission hall and a boys' club and, more recently, a Buddhist temple.*

Left: *Bury St Edmunds Theatre Royal, built by William Wilkins the younger in 1819, had rough usage as a barrel store for many years but returned to full theatre use in 1965.*

Left: *Many Georgian circuit theatres in country towns exist only as empty shells or barely recognisable fragments. Truro Theatre of c.1780 has one of the better-preserved exteriors.*

Five years later Wilkins's son, also William, who had taken over the Norwich circuit from his father, built the new Bury St Edmunds Theatre Royal. As might be expected from this distinguished neo-classical architect, who also designed Downing College, Cambridge, and the National Gallery in London, this is an elegant, geometrically disciplined design.

The decline in theatre attendance that set in in the 1820s and 1830s has been explained in a number of ways. Economic decline was the major cause, but growing boredom with an unchanging diet of second-rate drama was possibly also a factor. The writing was on the wall for the provincial circuits and, by the 1840s, many small theatres had fallen into disuse and dereliction. The spread of the railways, the continuing emigration of the rural population to industrial towns and the rise of touring companies that required larger theatres for their work finished the job. Before the end of the century most of the old circuit theatres had

*The Coburg Theatre, now known as the Old Vic, was built in 1818 to the designs of Rudolphe Cabanel. Much of the exterior is still original and the front elevation is a modern partial re-creation of this original restrained classical design.*

A View of the Old & New Haymarket Theatres

*Haymarket Theatre Royal by John Nash, 1821, replacing the 'little theatre in the Hay' (seen to the left). The present interior is much later in date, but the Nash façade remains a prominent London landmark.*

disappeared or been converted to houses, barrel stores or drill halls. The Chichester Theatre, which became a shop, is amongst those still recognisable from their surviving exteriors.

Urban theatre activity was more resilient. Some major theatres in populous centres began to aspire to a little of the architectural grandeur of their continental counterparts. Nash's Haymarket Theatre Royal of 1821 had a classical portico, closing the view from St James's Square. Grand porticoes also appeared on Samuel Beazley's Lyceum of 1834 and the Greens' Newcastle Theatre Royal of 1837.

One of the really big theatres of the time, Benjamin Dean Wyatt's Theatre Royal, Drury Lane, was built in 1812 to replace Henry Holland's splendid 1794 theatre, which had been destroyed by fire. It turned out to be a theatrical mess, demonstrating that the employment of a member of a famous architectural dynasty to design a beautiful building (and its auditorium was certainly beautiful) is not necessarily a recipe for

*Another landmark theatre portico is that of the Theatre Royal in Newcastle upon Tyne by John and Benjamin Green, 1837.*

*Benjamin Dean Wyatt's Drury Lane Theatre Royal of 1812 had its auditorium completely remodelled in 1822 and again in 1922, but it still has the grandest Georgian interiors to be seen in any British theatre. This is the Rotunda.*

producing a satisfactory theatre. The exterior seen today is largely Wyatt's, but the auditorium was redesigned in 1822 by Beazley, who also added the side colonnade. He was also a playwright and understood the needs of the drama. Beazley was Britain's first real specialist in theatre design. His work survived, with alterations, until 1922, when the auditorium was replaced by the present one.

The continued protection given to the patent houses determined, to a large extent, the character of theatrical fare elsewhere in the metropolis. The non-patent theatres, in order to stay precariously within the law, offered quasi-dramatic pieces accompanied by music (to a steadily lessening extent) and interspersed with songs. These performances were known as 'burlettas' and licensed as such (if licensed at all) by the Lord Chamberlain. This officer of the Royal Household was, in fact, responsible for defending the anachronistic privileges of the patent houses, but conditions had changed so radically by the 1830s that, despite the vigorous protests of the patentees, it was becoming obvious that the old order had to change.

*Samuel Beazley added a colonnade to the side of Drury Lane Theatre Royal in 1831.*

The Theatres Act of 1843 delivered the final blow to the patent theatres, allowing the Lord Chamberlain to grant a theatre licence to any suitable person. The patents became ornamental status symbols, conferring little in the way of profitable advantages. Even so, there was no immediate rush to build new theatres in London. There were enough theatres and near-theatres already on the ground – but the Act did have an unexpected side effect, leading to the building of entertainment houses of a rather different kind.

The bounding growth of the great urban centres at this time was producing a reverse effect to that observed in the country. A mighty thirst for spectacular and intellectually undemanding diversions could not be completely satisfied by the existing 'minors' (non-patent regular theatres), the circuses, the pleasure gardens or the cheaply built 'saloon' theatres attached to pubs.

The saloons were, in fact, doomed, since they relied on the sale of drink as their main source of profit. They could, theoretically, continue on a dramatic course with one of the Lord Chamberlain's new licences and one or two did so, but these licences forbade drinking in the auditorium. Most of the saloons could not survive under this restriction. They went under and much blood and thunder drama went with them.

Pub entertainment, however, survived and prospered. Proprietors soon saw the advantages of giving up dramatic ambition and opting instead for the kind of varied, mainly vocal, entertainments that could be presented with a music and dancing licence easily obtained from the magistrates. Crucially, magistrates' licences permitted drinking during the performance.

This kind of chairman-led non-dramatic fare was already long established in pub singing rooms and supper rooms, and it was growing in popularity. In the late 1840s and early 1850s purpose-built concert rooms were being attached to pubs wherever there was space to do so and the emergence of a new entertainment industry, the music hall, became inevitable.

*The Grand Harmonic Hall at the Grapes Tavern, Southwark, later known as the Winchester, was one of the first true music halls. It was built in 1846 but had begun to look small and old-fashioned by the 1860s. It was demolished about 1882.*

# The rise of music halls - 1851 to 1880

The Theatres Act may, accidentally, have created the conditions for the emergence of a new form of entertainment, but all the necessary ingredients had, in fact, been present in the minor theatres, the saloons and the pub concerts, well before 1843.

The hybrid dramatic fare that non-patent theatres had been able to present, with hornpipes and comic songs between the acts, may not have appealed to self-consciously respectable folk, but it was hugely popular and attracted big audiences. The variety content of their bills was readily woven into the fabric of the new entertainment. Pub concerts themselves became ever more ambitious, with operatic selections, ballads, and male and female comic singers 'in character'. The concerts were able to recruit some of their talent from the versatile actors and singers bred by the old theatrical regime.

The music hall movement gathered momentum rapidly. In 1854 Charles Morton, who had for two years been running an average-sized concert room attached to his Lambeth pub, acquired a number of adjoining properties and built a new music hall. This, his second Canterbury Hall, completed in 1855, was a giant, much bigger than anything ever seen before. He poached the best talent from the theatres, opera houses, Covent Garden supper rooms, concert rooms and pleasure gardens, achieving such spectacular success that his example was quickly

*The second Canterbury Hall, built behind a little pub in Lambeth, opened before completion in 1855, was the first of the giant supper room music halls that began to appear in London in the 1850s and 1860s. It was subsequently rebuilt as a variety theatre and later demolished after bombing.*

followed. Early imitators were Paddy Green, who built a new hall at the long-established Evans's in Covent Garden, 1856, Edward Weston in Holborn, 1857, and John Wilton in Stepney, 1859. A succession of other proprietors went on building this type of hall into the 1870s.

These early 'grand music halls', although as big as, or bigger than, regular theatres, had a marked character of their own, closer to bar room than to theatre. They were flat-floored, brilliantly lit rooms, often with a simple platform stage and a balcony at the end, or on three sides. There was at least one bar and servery open to the hall. The floor was covered with lines of dining tables, with rows of benches farther from the stage and a wide promenade on all sides. The audience came and went, as in a pub, eating and drinking and meeting friends, while being entertained by mainly vocal turns announced by a chairman who sat at the top table, in front of the stage.

The movement was not limited to London. All the major cities had music halls of this kind. The extraordinary thing is that so little visible evidence of this early period now remains. Wilton's (The Old Mahogany Bar) in London and the

Above: *A typical music hall bar, open to the auditorium. Note that hats and outdoor clothes are worn, as in a pub, and the promenade is full of standing figures.*

*The chairman was essential in the earlier music halls (this is an 1874 example), to keep order, to announce the artistes and to ensure that there were ample opportunities to serve food and drink in the hall between the turns.*

*Even after drinking was removed from the auditorium and music halls began to be more like theatres, the gallery could still be boisterous at times.*

Right: *The pit in a late-Victorian variety theatre with a contortionist on stage: 'Auntie, can you do that?' The later variety houses had no chairman, the acts being identified by a number in a frame at the side of the stage.*

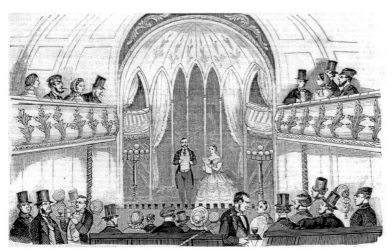

*Wilton's Music Hall in Stepney, in the East End of London, 1859, also known as the Old Mahogany Bar, is the sole survivor of the Canterbury-style London music halls. It was reconstructed in 1878 after a fire but still retains its primitive supper room form.*

*The Britannia Music Hall in Glasgow, of 1859/60 (seen here c.2001), is a remarkably complete representative of the early period of music hall development. After long years of disuse the temporary roof-like structure over the pit has now been removed.*

Britannia in Glasgow are the only nearly intact examples of the giant supper room halls of the 1850s. When the music halls moved into London's West End, notably with Morton's Oxford in 1861, the theatres felt threatened by the competition.

Some regular theatres were built or rebuilt during this period, but the survival rate, particularly of interiors, has, again, been poor, since many were totally reconstructed later. Significant representatives still to be seen from this era are the Royal Italian Opera House, Covent Garden, rebuilt in 1858 after a fire, the Tyne Theatre and Opera House of 1867 in

Left: *Leeds City Varieties, formerly known as Thornton's. Like the Glasgow Britannia, it is at first-floor level, built above the White Swan Tavern in 1865. The upper balcony was extended along the side walls, probably in the 1880s.*

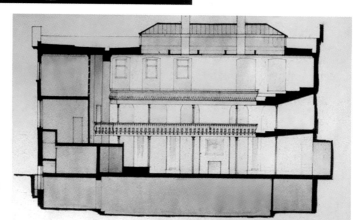

*Hoxton Hall is a small London music hall which, unusually, was never attached to a pub. Built in 1863, the roof was raised and an upper balcony added in 1867.*

*Edward Barry's Royal Italian Opera House, Covent Garden, opened in 1858. It incorporated fine sculptural figures and reliefs from its predecessor.*

*Barry's auditorium in what is now the Royal Opera House is architecturally unique in Britain. A huge development programme incorporating Barry's building was completed in 1999.*

*The original Old Vic auditorium by Cabanel was replaced in 1871. After many subsequent alterations the 1871 auditorium was restored to its original appearance in 1983.*

Newcastle, the Old Vic, 1871, the Criterion, 1874 and 1884 (London's first completely subterranean theatre), and Glasgow's Citizen's, 1878.

This period saw the appearance of the first specialist theatre architects since Beazley, namely Jethro T. Robinson, Thomas Verity, C. J. Phipps and Walter Emden. Of these, Phipps was easily the most productive, with at least forty new theatres and more than twenty other rebuilds or transformations to his credit.

Determined efforts were made by managements at this time to win back a middle-class audience. The plays they offered were intended to give pleasure without offending sensibilities, and the theatres themselves were designed with the same end in view. C. J. Phipps, in particular, created dignified auditoria and public spaces in which people who would once have hesitated to enter any place as socially undesirable as a theatre could feel completely at home. Phipps's Bath Theatre Royal auditorium of 1863 and his Edinburgh Royal Lyceum of 1883 exemplify this trend.

Left: *Margate Theatre Royal has an almost perfectly preserved auditorium of 1874 by J. T. Robinson (who designed the Old Vic auditorium) within a partly Georgian outer shell.*

Above: *The first of the great Victorian specialist theatre architects, C. J. Phipps (1835–97). More than sixty theatres were designed or completely redesigned by him.*

Left: *William Parnell's 1867 auditorium in the Tyne Theatre and Opera House, Newcastle upon Tyne, now shows evidence of some later alterations but is otherwise a rare survival of its period.*

*Leeds Grand Theatre and Opera House, by Corson & Watson, 1878, has an auditorium that must rate as one of the most spectacular in Britain. Its free Gothic style is unique.*

*Bath Theatre Royal, as rebuilt in 1863 after a fire, was the first theatre designed by C. J. Phipps, who went on to become the leading theatre architect of his time. This interior set a pattern which was developed in many of his later works.*

Perhaps the most remarkable surviving example of the movement toward comfortable respectability was Corson & Watson's Leeds Grand Opera House of 1878. This spectacular theatre, initiated by a group of local industrialists rather than by theatre entrepreneurs, is on a scale rarely seen at any time in Britain and in a style otherwise completely unrepresented – a blend of Romanesque and Gothic.

During the 1860s the music halls, born in working-class areas like Lambeth, quickly moved into city centres, where they stood face to face with the theatres. The larger halls, like the Alhambra in Leicester Square, issued a direct challenge by adopting the ballet, which, after its romantic heyday, had been abandoned by the opera houses. The *ballets d'action* at the Alhambra, the Metropolitan and later the Leicester Square Empire

Below left: *The major music hall stages had to be designed (or redesigned) to accommodate dance. The Empire in Leicester Square, rival to the Alhambra, had a magnificent interior. This view is dated 1894.*

Below right: *The Empire featured the great ballerina Adeline Genée (seen here c.1905).*

*Ballet was kept alive in the music halls after it was abandoned by the opera houses. The Alhambra, converted from the Leicester Square Panopticon, became one of the great mid-Victorian music halls and a home to lavish ballet productions. This fine lithograph shows it in the mid 1860s, with the audience sitting at supper tables. Leicester Square Odeon cinema now stands on the site.*

*Before the 1890s the life of a theatre commonly ended with a fire. One of the more spectacular events was the burning of Her Majesty's Theatre in London in 1867.*

may not have been epoch-making, but they kept the art alive, provided employment for dancers and choreographers and, as importantly, kept a ballet audience in existence until the arrival of the *Ballets Russes* in the twentieth century.

The last years of this period saw music hall architecture beginning to move hesitantly toward regular theatre form. Open concert platforms were replaced by proscenium stages designed, wherever space permitted, to accommodate ballets. Capacity was increased by cutting down on the number of supper tables and increasing the size of the benched areas.

The process of convergence was pushed along by the imposition of safety controls. These began to be evident around 1880 (in London after the Metropolis Management Act of 1878). Deaths caused by fire in gas-lit theatres and other places of public assembly (or, as often, caused by attempted escape, whether or not a fire had actually broken out), were appallingly numerous in the early and middle years of the nineteenth century. After many years of official apathy and management resistance, it came to be recognised at last that theatres must be designed to allow the audience at every level to leave the building quickly and in an orderly manner at the first sign of danger. Useless attempts to devise ways of making the buildings totally fireproof or to incorporate fallible devices for dousing flames made way for simple, intelligent planning.

The controls were slow to bite at first, but the basic truths underlying them, based on observation of audience behaviour and the provision of adequate means for their escape, were applied to music halls and theatres alike. The effects were observable in the next period.

# Heyday - 1881 to 1916

The next thirty-five years saw an unprecedented boom in theatre building, fuelled by the demands of a burgeoning urban population. In mid-Victorian times the building of a theatre or a music hall had commonly been a matter of individual or small company enterprise. The early music halls, in particular, often bore the names of their proprietors, as with Weston's, Wilton's and Harwood's in London, Thornton's in Leeds (now City Varieties) and Day's Crystal Palace in Birmingham. The new surge of building, however, was largely powered by well-financed syndicates who, by attracting the investments of speculators great and small, were able to create chains of touring houses across Britain.

They compressed the old music hall programmes that had lasted the whole evening into two or three hours and eventually into two or even three shows a night. As the power of the syndicates grew they were able to dictate terms and conditions to performers, treating the lesser lights as if they were hired hands and barring them from appearing at competing halls. Such behaviour was reasonably seen by the victims as bullying, but managers were riding the crest of a wave. They were all but impregnable. Theatre was economically a thoroughly healthy business and variety was a huge money-maker by the 1890s.

The profit pressure behind the boom was accompanied by an even tougher regime of official inspections and a steady screwing down of safety controls. Many old theatres failed to make the grade and had to be rebuilt. Nearly all backland pub music halls, no matter how profitable they had been, were condemned as potential death traps. Some were rebuilt on theatrical lines but hundreds of lesser halls simply disappeared, to the further benefit of the variety palace builders.

*Haymarket Theatre: detail of paintings by Harker, 1905, restored 1994.*

Above: *Dan Leno and Herbert Campbell, the famous music hall and pantomime partnership, built three variety houses but could not compete with the powerful syndicates.*

*Douglas Gaiety: act drop by William Hemsley, 1900, restored 1992.*

# Alhambra Theatre,

CHARING CROSS ROAD and LEICESTER SQUARE.

. . THE . .

NATIONAL THEATRE
OF
VARIETIES.

General Manager .. C. DUNDAS SLATER.

Acting Manager, Mr. E. A. PICKERING.
Sec. and Treas., Mr. H WOODFORD.

Stage Manager, Mr. CHAS. WILSON
Musical Director, Mr. GEO. W. BYNG

## PROGRAMME

Subject to alterations at the discretion of the Management.

### For MONDAY, SEPTEMBER 1st, 1902, and during the Week.

| | | |
|---|---|---|
| 1. | OVERTURE | 7.55 |
| | MARCH ... "The King's Jester" Carl Mertoni | |

| | | |
|---|---|---|
| 2. | PHŒNIX TRIO, Equilibrists. | 8.0 |

| | | |
|---|---|---|
| 3. | MISS MARY DESMOND, Ballad Vocalist. | 8.10 |

4. A New Fantastic Ballet Divertissement, 8.20
entitled—

## IN JAPAN

Adapted by S. L. Bensusan, from his Story "Dédé."*
MUSIC SPECIALLY COMPOSED BY M. LOUIS GANNE.
Costumes by ALIAS, from Designs by COMELLI. Scenery by PHILIP HOWDEN.
Properties by LAUREYS. Electrician, WEBBER. Machinist, Fox.
Wigs by GUSTAVE. Floral Decorations by GATTI.
Dances by Signor CARLO COPPI. Produced by CHARLES WILSON
and Signor COPPI.

Under the direction of C. DUNDAS SLATER.

CAST.

| | | |
|---|---|---|
| Prince Korin | Governor of Province | Mr. TOM COVENTRY |
| Two Japanese Officials | | Mr ARTELLI and Mr. APPLEBY |
| Shimbun | First Guide | Mr. F. FAIREN |
| Sosen | Second Guide | Mr. E. ALMONTI |
| Foreign Visitors | | Mr. A. WALCOTT |
| | A Country Girl | Miss R. DEANE |
| Dédé | A Geisha | Miss N. H UGHTON |
| Maiko | | Miss L. DUNBAR |
| Koyuki | | Miss A. LOGAN |
| Kikou | | Miss BURGESS |
| Okanisan | Mistress of the Tea House. | |
| Torio | Japanese boy Lover of Dédé | Miss SLACK |

Geisha, Samourais, Guides, Beggars, Ricksha Drivers, etc., etc.

* The Story of Dédé was published in the "Sketch."

| | | |
|---|---|---|
| 5. | Mr. JOE O'GORMAN, Irish Comedian. | 8.45 |

| | | |
|---|---|---|
| 6. | ORCHESTRAL SELECTION | 8.55 |
| | "Mikado" ... Sullivan | |

| | | |
|---|---|---|
| 7. | KRASUCKI'S MONKEYS. | 9.5 |
| | First Appearance in London. | |

8. THE WORLD'S EVENTS 9.20
Reproduced by THE IMPERIAL BIOSCOPE.
Invented by C. URBAN, London, under the direction of The Alhambra.
THE CORONATION.
The privilege of witnessing the Coronation Procession on the historic 9th was only for the minority, but the wonders of science have made a view of the memorable pageant possible to all. By an exclusive arrangement the Alhambra Theatre have secured and are at present showing a series of moving pictures which for length, clearness of detail and point of view, is probably the finest ever secured of any event of national interest.

| | | |
|---|---|---|
| 9. | LES BRUNIN, Eccentric Billiardists. | 9.40 |

| | | |
|---|---|---|
| 10. | MUSICAL DALE, Campanologist. | 9.55 |

| | | |
|---|---|---|
| 11. | LA BELLE GUERRERO, | 10.5 |
| | The beautiful Spanish Danseuse. | |

12. A New Grand Spectacular Ballet, entitled— 10.20

## BRITANNIA'S REALM

IN PROLOGUE AND FOUR SCENES.

Invented and Produced by CHARLES WILSON.
Music Specially Composed by LANDON RONALD.
Dances arranged by Signor CARLO COPPI.
Costumes by ALIAS, from Designs by COMELLI. Properties by LAUREYS.
Electrician, WEBBER. Machinist, Fox.
Wigs by GUSTAVE. Floral Decorations by GATTI.
The whole Produced under the direction of C. DUNDAS SLATER.

| | | |
|---|---|---|
| Prologue | .. "The Abode of Fame" | ..Philip Howden |
| Scene 1.—AFRICA | .. "The Soudan." | ..Phl'ip Howden |
| „ 2.—INDIA | | ..E. H. Ryan, junr. |
| „ 3.—AUSTRALIA | | ..E. H. Ryan, junr. |
| „ 4.—CANADA | | ..E. H. Ryan, junr. |

CAST.

PROLOGUE.—THE HALL OF FAME.

| | | |
|---|---|---|
| Britannia | | Miss BLANEY |
| Malice | | Miss E. SLACK |
| Envy | | Miss J. REEVE |
| Justice | | Miss M. HUNT |
| Father Time | | Mr. G. ALMONTI |

SCENE 1.—THE SOUDAN.

| | | |
|---|---|---|
| A Native Woman | | Miss BURGESS |
| Her Two Children | | Miss MARRA |
| | | Miss L. BAKER |
| A Slave Dealer | | Mr. WALCOTT |

SCENE 2.—INDIA.

| | | |
|---|---|---|
| Grand March.. | "The Rajah and his retinue " | |
| Dances | .. "Fauns and Lotus " | |
| Sapphire | | Miss N. HOUGHTON and Corps de Ballet |
| Pearl | | Miss L. BIRCHAM „ „ „ |
| Turquoise | | Miss A. LOGAN „ „ „ |
| Ruby | | Miss ADA TAYLOR „ „ „ |
| | AND | |
| Diamond | | Miss E. SLACK |

SCENE 3.—AUSTRALIA. "True to the Motherland!"

| | | |
|---|---|---|
| The Mother | | Madame CORMANI |
| The Daughter | | Miss ROSIE DEANE |
| Her Soldier Lover | | Mr. G. ALMONTI |
| The Son | | Miss JULIA REEVE |
| The Father | | Mr. T. COVENTRY |

SCENE 4.—CANADA—SKATING CARNIVAL.

| | | |
|---|---|---|
| Dance | | Mr. F. FAIREN |
| | | Messrs. F. FAIREN & TOWHEY |
| Pas des Patineurs | | Mesdames BERNARD, TAYL IR, |
| Valse | | J. MEYERS, D'ANVILLE, and |
| Galop. | | Corps de Ballet |
| Première Danseuse | | Mdlle. ALMA MARI |

GRAND FINALE.

HOMAGE TO BRITANNIA. The Crosses of St. Patrick, St. Andrew and St. George forming the Union Jack of Old England.

| | | |
|---|---|---|
| 13. | POLK and KOLLINS, Banjoists. | 11.5 |

| | | |
|---|---|---|
| 14. | MDLLE. ALICE on the Revolving Trapeze. | 11.15 |

A combination of these regulatory pressures and changing public expectations completed the architectural convergence of the two building types. The new variety palaces and the 'straight' theatres of the 1890s differed from one another only in the nature of the entertainment on the stage and the comparative brashness or sobriety of their ornament.

Theatre audiences now expected to be a great deal safer and more comfortable than they had been in the past. Variety audiences had similar expectations, but they were to experience even greater changes. Controlling authorities, many of whom were as concerned with clamping down on immorality and liquor consumption as they were with audience safety, were bent on eliminating the old style halls with their free, boozy

*A variety bill of 1902 with the bioscope presented as a 'turn'. Even the coronation of Edward VII rated only a twenty-minute spot, but the 'bio' was a cuckoo that was eventually to take over the nest.*

atmosphere, and this they achieved in a remarkably short time.

The new variety theatres (correctly so-called, although the term 'music hall' lingered on well into the twentieth century) were places for the family. Members of the audience paid for admission and sat in fixed seats, as in a playhouse, for the length of the programme. The pub ambience had gone for ever. Drinking was limited to the bars and mainly to the intervals and no bar was permitted within the auditorium (although some bars did, for a time, have a clear view of the stage through a glass screen).

The building boom called into existence a new generation of specialist architects who knew how theatres worked and could thread their way through the regulatory maze. They were not highly regarded by the

*The Apollo by Lewen Sharp, 1901, has a finely modelled façade with a Parisian flavour, unlike any other London theatre.*

mainstream of the architectural profession, who saw them as commercial hacks, but they created superb interiors, with an abundance of theatrical atmosphere. The best of their gorgeous inventions have rarely been equalled and never surpassed by later theatre architects. The leader of the movement, Frank Matcham, who succeeded to J. T. Robinson's practice, designed or totally transformed at least a hundred and twenty theatres (the true total may never be known).

The theatres of this period were still rigidly divided, with separate entrances, seating areas and bars, so that upper-class, middle-class and working-class patrons need never meet. The pittites and galleryites were still crammed on to undivided benches, while the carriage folk had their upholstered, tip-up armchairs in stalls and dress circle, but Matcham, for one, ensured that practically every seat, from the cheapest to the dearest, had a good view of the stage.

Matcham is still a byword for good theatre planning and opulent architectural treatment, but he was by no means alone.

Above: *The John Nash Theatre Royal, Haymarket, 1821, contains a much later auditorium, 1905, by C. Stanley Peach and S. D. Adshead.*

*Frank Matcham (1854–1920) was the presiding genius of the late-Victorian and Edwardian theatre building boom.*

*Harrogate Royal
Hall (formerly
Kursaal), 1903:
an example of the
finely detailed
work of
Matcham's
draughtsmen.*

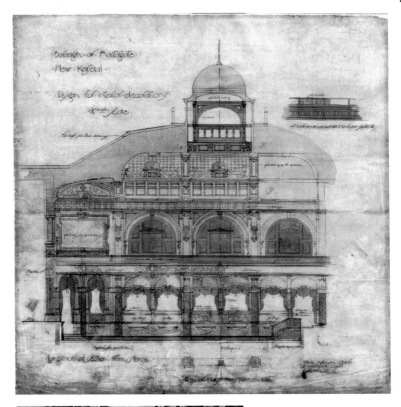

*Belfast Grand Opera House, by
Matcham, 1895, reopened in
1980 after extensive restoration
and improvement. The elephant
head ornaments are a reminder
that the design was at first
intended for a circus.*

*Wakefield Theatre Royal and Opera House, 1894, is the smallest of Frank Matcham's surviving theatres.*

His London contemporaries, Bertie Crewe and W. G. R. Sprague, produced magnificent theatres, as did the Birmingham practice of Owen & Ward and the north-eastern firm of Hope & Maxwell. Some of the architects of this period, like the shadowy J. J. Alley, who designed (or perhaps 'fronted') exclusively for the Broadhead circuit around Manchester and Liverpool, have yet to be given the attention they deserve.

The period was hugely productive in all forms of entertainment architecture. The great fun resort of Blackpool continued to add to its impressive Winter Gardens complex, which had opened in the 1870s. From 1894, the Winter Gardens met powerful competition from the Blackpool Tower development. Among the great rooms created in Blackpool at this time, Wylson & Long's splendid Winter Gardens Pavilion auditorium of 1897, Frank Matcham's Tower Circus of 1894 and his Tower Ballroom of 1899 are outstanding. The Ballroom is, indeed, one of the finest rooms of any kind built in Britain in the 1890s.

By the outbreak of the First World War variety entrepreneurs, like Moss, Thornton, Stoll, Broadhead, Howard & Wyndham and Barrasford, had built hundreds of lavish entertainment houses in every town and inner suburb. At the peak there were about a thousand active professional theatres in Britain. Major conurbations like Glasgow, Liverpool and Manchester had their own buzzing entertainment honeypots but, as might be expected, London boasted the greatest single concentration.

*Manchester Palace has an unprepossessing exterior, but its auditorium, as remodelled in 1913, represents its architect, Bertie Crewe, at his confident best.*

*Blackpool Grand, 1894. An entertaining exterior containing one of Matcham's most successful auditorium designs.*

*The Lyric by C. J. Phipps was the third theatre built on Shaftesbury Avenue in 1888. The exterior, like other Phipps theatres, was almost domestic in scale, but his auditorium was rich in atmosphere.*

A restructuring of the capital's road network took place over the whole period, changing the face of the West End and shifting the focus of both its day and night life. New highways such as Charing Cross Road, Shaftesbury Avenue, the Aldwych, Kingsway and the widened Strand were cut through densely populated and decaying areas, creating in the process prime development frontages at precisely the time that theatre enterprises were at a peak of profitability. It defies imagination today that any property developer would even think of building a theatre on a new

*Shaftesbury Avenue was cut in the mid 1880s, when theatre was approaching its most profitable period. The first buildings erected were theatres and, although one or two have been lost, the cluster of theatres on the Avenue defines the heart of present-day Theatreland.*

*Richard D'Oyly Carte built his Royal English Opera House as an architectural monument on an island site in central London in 1891. English opera failed and the building was converted to the Palace Theatre of Varieties. It is now a home for large-scale musicals.*

site in central London, but this is how Theatreland, as we now know it, emerged. The extraordinary conditions that led to its creation will never recur.

It is an interesting reflection on the cultural climate of the time that, whilst the big entertainment houses, offering opera, ballet, musical comedy and spectacle, were prospering, there was also a healthy demand for drama. Many of the buildings that made up the new Theatreland were playhouses, squeezed on to the smallest possible sites by feats of cunning planning. One architect, W. G. R. Sprague, who was also responsible for the Sheffield Lyceum, designed no fewer than eight of them between 1899 and 1916. His theatres may have made many compromises, cramming in extra seats to the detriment of good sightlines, and they may have lacked the sheer ebullience of those of Frank Matcham, but his interiors have rarely been equalled for elegance. Wyndham's was perhaps the most beautiful of his many inventions.

*W. G. R. Sprague (1865–1933) was a leading theatre architect whose trademark was elegance, contrasting with Matcham's ebullience.*

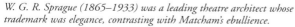

*Wyndham's auditorium of 1899 is one of the finest examples of W. G. R. Sprague's elegant theatre interiors.*

The most noticeable difference between the theatres at the beginning and end of this period was in the nature of their modelling and decoration. New modes of construction eventually released architects from the rigid discipline that cast-iron columns, timber beams and trusses had imposed on theatre design in the past, but the new spirit was evident before steel long-span beams became the norm.

J. T. Robinson, C. J. Phipps and Thomas Verity had moved slowly toward a greater degree of opulence and innovation in their interiors, but

*Sheffield Lyceum, by Sprague, 1897, was magnificently restored in 1990 after a decade of disuse and neglect.*

their designs still had their roots in an earlier tradition. Phipps, a prolific theatre designer, discovered a workable, pleasing and instantly recognisable form early in his career and continued to play variations on it throughout his working life. The new generation of designers adopted a much freer approach. Matcham, in particular, was quite incapable of repeating himself. Every theatre of his seemed to have been designed as a 'one-off'. His variety houses took decorative fantasy about as far as it could go, mingling baroque, rococo, Indian and other exotic motifs with apparent abandon, and yet with complete command. For theatrical

*The elegant Criterion Theatre by Thomas Verity, 1874 and 1884, in Piccadilly Circus, is wholly below ground. Its staircases and bars are handsomely decorated with Minton tiles.*

*The Gaiety in Douglas, Isle of Man, is a brilliant conversion by Frank Matcham, 1900, of an arched, glazed pavilion. His magnificently decorated interiors and machined stage have been restored with archaeological precision.*

*His Majesty's in Aberdeen is one of Frank Matcham's later theatres. Built in 1906, it is faced with silvery grey granite.*

atmosphere there has been little in the world to compare with the best work of this period. And yet, beyond their surface appearance, these magnificent interiors were actually models of efficient, logical design.

The introduction in the 1890s of steel 'cantilevered' balconies, spanning the auditorium without intrusive columns, greatly benefited the audience, not least those in the cheaper seats. Various kinds of reinforced concrete began to be introduced even earlier than steel construction, but the material was not until many years later exploited by theatre designers, as one might have expected it to be, for its plastic qualities. It tended to be used as a simple replacement for traditional materials. What was exploited was its fire-resisting quality which, at the time, would have been viewed as its main advantage.

It is often the case that seemingly unstoppable historical movements come to a climax and a rapid end in quick succession. The surge of theatre building in Britain reached its peak at the beginning of the twentieth century. By 1916 it was all over. One reason, certainly, was that provision had finally satisfied demand, but a close look at the late variety

*Matcham's last major theatre was Bristol Hippo-drome, 1912, a variety house designed to serve also as a circus, with a floodable arena.*

The greatest of all Matcham's theatres was the London Coliseum, built as a variety house for Oswald Stoll in 1904. The restored tower is a London landmark. The auditorium is of Roman grandeur. This is now the home of English National Opera.

*Sir Oswald Stoll (1866–1942), the variety theatre magnate and builder of the London Coliseum.*

houses, in particular, will show that they contained an infection that was to prove fatal.

Motion pictures arrived in Britain quietly enough with an exhibition of the Lumière system at the Regent Street Polytechnic Institute in 1896. Allen Eyles in *Old Cinemas* (Shire, new edition 2011) has mapped the progress of the new entertainment form and the buildings that served it. All that is needed here is to note the effects on theatre architecture.

To take only two telling examples, both designed by Frank Matcham for Stoll, the Hackney Empire of 1901 had a projection room from the beginning. Similarly, the immense London Coliseum of 1904, the most ambitious variety theatre ever built, far more suitable for its present-day use as an opera and dance house than for music hall artistes, had purpose-built projection rooms.

Films were by now a regular part of the variety programme and ad hoc arrangements would no longer do. The risk posed by early celluloid film led in 1909 to a legal requirement for fire-separated projection rooms and this led in turn to the immediate closure of many makeshift picture houses. Matcham, having provided film with a more or less safe home eight years earlier, actually helped to start a process which eventually wiped out hundreds of live theatres.

The first of the new, dedicated picture houses were rectangular, flat-walled, tunnel-vaulted rooms, often with vestigial stages for live acts between the films. The turns tended to be third-rate, but the growing popularity of these 'cine-varieties' contributed heavily to the rapid rise of the cinemas and the slow but inexorable decline of the variety houses.

# The First World War to 1950

The next thirty-five years were essentially the age of the cinema, which went from strength to strength, culminating in the lavish 'supers' and the 'atmospherics' of the 1930s. All over Britain, these super cinemas with fully equipped stages for live performance (no longer second-grade turns) made the local Empires and Hippodromes look hopelessly old-fashioned. Despite this dominating trend, a completely unsignalled 'little boom' in theatre building occurred, with a sharp peak in 1930. This phenomenon, it must be said, was practically limited to London's West End.

The most advanced experimentation in theatre design was being conducted on the continent, but this made little impact on British commercial theatre design, even in the capital. The Drury Lane auditorium was rebuilt in 1922, but this was still essentially a Georgian theatre in new make-up. The new auditorium was also backward-looking, the last of its kind, rather than the first of a rising generation. By contrast, just two years later, its near neighbour, the modest little Fortune, broke away completely from the old style. The almost undecorated concrete façade and the box-like auditorium did not in any way amount to a revolutionary design, but the Fortune marked a stylistic turning point in what remained a thoroughly uncertain time for theatre design.

Although the rebuilt Savoy, 1929, the Adelphi, 1930, and the little Whitehall, 1930, adopted the latest fashions in decoration, they were

*Edinburgh Playhouse by John Fairweather, a super cinema of 1929, shows the influence of American cinema design. Like many of its kind it has a practical theatre stage.*

*Drury Lane Theatre Royal: the 1922 auditorium, by Walker, Jones & Cromie, was one of the last to be designed in the opulent manner of the previous generation of theatre buildings.*

*The Fortune, 1924, by Ernest Shaufelberg, was the first completely new West End theatre built after the First World War. The interior represented a significant departure from the turn-of-the-century style.*

not, by any means, marching with the architectural or theatrical avant-garde. The Phoenix, 1930, was a modern variant on the traditional multi-tiered form, dressed up in vivid new style by a decorator who was later to become famous for his extravagant cinema designs.

Some theatres at this time, like the Dominion, 1929, were designed for instant conversion to cinema if that proved to be the most profitable route to take, but even those intended for permanent theatre use had to be designed with sightlines to suit projected images. This was a technology which, once available to the theatre, could simply not be ignored. The *fin-de-siècle* style, with balconies curved round to link with stacks of boxes framing the proscenium, produced a warmth of embrace which was quite unsuitable for viewing flat images. Rows of seats eventually became nearly straight and there was no longer any sense of 'papering the walls with people'. In the cinemas, the intimidating effect

*The interior of the Savoy, as remodelled in 1929 by Frank Tugwell and Basil Ionides, is a tour de force of Art Deco.*

*The New Victoria (now Apollo Victoria) by E. Wamsley Lewis & W. E. Trent, 1929, another super cinema with a theatrical stage, has become a musical house.*

Right: *The illuminated tower of the Prince of Wales, by Robert Cromie, 1937, was a London example of the 'architecture of night', particularly popular in Germany in the previous decade.*

of bare side walls was mitigated by turning them into an architectural and decorative playground which often relied as much on lighting effects as on modelling or art decoration.

The Stratford-upon-Avon new Shakespeare Memorial Theatre of 1932 was, perhaps, the most prominent example of a theatre design deeply flawed by the uncertainties of the time. The original auditorium had to be continually modified in a struggle to achieve a more satisfactory form. The eventual solution, completed in 2010, was a total reconstruction.

By 1950, variety, which had been the great energiser of the previous period, was running down rapidly. Those variety houses that had not been converted to dismally unsatisfactory cinemas were dead on their feet. The big operators who owned them were busy selling them off as bingo houses or, where land values were high, as development sites.

*Stratford-upon-Avon, Royal Shakespeare Theatre: Elisabeth Scott's new Shakespeare Memorial Theatre, seen here in 1932, was praised by architectural critics but proved to be theatrically dispiriting. The auditorium underwent many alterations before being completely redesigned in 2010.*

# The great theatre massacre - and after

An authoritative work published in 1982 (*Curtains!!! or A New Life for Old Theatres*) estimated that 85 per cent of the thousand or so theatres that had existed in 1914, most of them active at that time, had been demolished or mutilated beyond recall by 1980. *Curtains!!!* identified 166 surviving pre-1914 theatres in its top three quality ratings, of which only ninety-seven were in active theatre use at the date of publication. The more appalling statistic is that the worst of these losses occurred in just two decades, from 1955 to 1975.

After the Second World War with cinema, and later television, seducing once-loyal audiences, theatre doors closed everywhere. Retreat became a rout, the axe falling not where society had judged that pruning and careful renewal might be advisable, but where developers' economics dictated. The best theatres on prime sites were often the first to go, but

*Newbury and Speenhamland, Berkshire: a Georgian circuit theatre of 1802, whose substantial remains were wantonly destroyed in the 1960s.*

*Bertie Crewe's magnificent London Opera House of 1911, later called the Stoll Theatre, was lost in the 1960s at the height of the post-war theatre massacre.*

even in suburbs where development pressure was low demolition was almost the rule, a cleansing act of destruction being seen as a sort of passport to progress.

The fortunate theatres were the ones that found a future in a new commercial use – most often bingo. Bingo was reasonably amenable, requiring little in the way of physical change, but later pressures for conversion to nightclubs and discotheques were more dangerous, requiring elimination of stalls rakes and the insertion of flat floors extending into the stage area.

The great theatre massacre left many cities with only two or three surviving old theatres where there may have been a dozen. Smaller towns and most suburbs often finished up with no theatres at all.

Below: *Leicester Theatre Royal was a fine theatre whose demolition in the uncaring post-war years seems now to have been extremely short-sighted and wasteful.*

*The Star in Bermondsey was one of the last surviving examples of a transitional music hall halfway between a pub hall and a variety theatre. Its rarity passed unnoticed when it was demolished in 1963.*

Hardly any old theatres were protected by inclusion in the statutory lists of historic buildings until the late 1970s. The exceptions, such as the Theatres Royal Drury Lane and Haymarket, simply served to underline the fact that only historically obvious candidates had been considered. The great boom theatres had not even been looked at.

There was a late but inevitable reaction. The loss of Frank Matcham's Granville Theatre in Walham Green in 1971 shocked those who saw its gorgeous interior being shattered and this led to action by the Greater London Council. Pressure on the responsible Secretary of State led to eighteen theatres being added to the London lists within two years and the process has since continued nationwide. The great theatres of the past were at last recognised as an important part of Britain's national heritage.

Listing halted the destructive trend and made it possible to safeguard the physical attributes of old theatres, but the protection of theatre buildings as cultural resources (rather than heritage objects) had to wait a little longer. A private member's measure, The Theatres Trust Act of

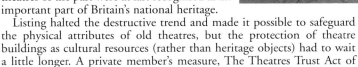

*Great Yarmouth Hippodrome of 1903, by R. S. Cockrill, is a remarkable survivor, one of only two purpose-built circuses still working in Britain.*

*Blackpool Grand, by Frank Matcham, 1894, was a redundant bingo house on the brink of demolition in 1973. Its rescue by local activists and subsequent success as a live theatre was one of the earliest indications of the turn of the tide of post-war destruction.*

Below left: *Hackney Empire, 1901, is one of Matcham's most imaginative designs, restored to active life after long years of non-theatre use.*

1976, passed with all-party support, created a new body charged with 'the better protection of theatres for the benefit of the nation'. The Theatres Trust is now recognised by all as the national advocate for theatre buildings, new and old, listed and unlisted.

Despite all the losses that occurred, there were still in the 1970s a remarkable number of 'sleeping beauties', fine theatres in non-theatre uses or no use at all, that could be kissed back to life if there was sufficient determination to do so. One of the early revivals snatched from imminent demolition was the Blackpool Grand, but the list of such successes has grown annually. Bradford Alhambra, to take only one example, was for many years earmarked as a site for a city centre car park. It is now an important regional theatre.

The restoration of old theatres has had a noticeably beneficial effect on the design of modern theatres. In the post-war decades many local authorities built bald and unattractive civic theatres that were actually multi-purpose rooms. A good theatre can be pressed into a variety of

*The little opera house in Craig-y-Nos Castle, Powys, built for Adelina Patti in 1891, is an intact Victorian private theatre.*

*Unusual, even among modern theatres, the New Vic in Newcastle-under-Lyme, Staffordshire, 1984, is purpose-built for theatre-in-the-round.*

*Above: The Royal National Theatre, 1976, by Sir Denys Lasdun, has a monumental architectural presence.*

temporary uses, but a room designed for a multiplicity of purposes rarely makes a good theatre. Some of these new buildings were actually built within walking distance of old theatres that could have given better service.

Against this generally dispiriting background, Peter Moro's Nottingham Playhouse, 1963, Elder Lester & Partners' Billingham Forum, 1968, Roderick Ham's Leatherhead Thorndike, 1969, and RHWL's Crucible at Sheffield, 1971, all shine out as innovative designs. They signalled a renaissance that has produced new theatres of many different types, ranging from Denys Lasdun's monumental Royal National Theatre in 1976 to the revolutionary Royal Exchange Theatre by

*The Royal National foyers are seductive spaces in themselves.*

*Manchester Royal Exchange, 1976 and 1999, by Levitt Bernstein, is one of the most revolutionary theatre designs of its time, a theatre-in-the-round contained in a free-standing structure within a much older building.*

Levitt Bernstein, 1976 – a 'lunar module' sitting inside Manchester's former Cotton Exchange – and countless smaller ones, like Nicoll Russell Studios' Byre Theatre in St Andrews, 2001.

New familiarity with the designs of the theatre architects of earlier times has led to a sharpened awareness of what makes a good theatre.

*The Tricycle, 1980 and 1989, has a plain scaffold structure adapting the deceptively simple geometry of a Georgian circuit theatre.*

*The new Glyndebourne Opera House, Lewes, Sussex, 1994: a wholly modern design whose underlying geometry reflects the virtues of earlier theatre forms.*

Theatre architects of today, without copying the past, have rediscovered their roots. Early courtyard theatres have inspired the form of smaller houses like Bill Howell's Christ's Hospital theatre, 1974, in Horsham and the Cottesloe, 1976, a highly influential design conceived by Iain Mackintosh as the third space in Lasdun's National complex. The London Tricycle, a courtyard design by Tim Foster (with Mackintosh), 1980, rebuilt in 1989 after a fire, is completely modern in expression but adopts the underlying geometry of a Georgian circuit theatre. Another well-tested traditional form, the horseshoe plan, has influenced the design of, for example, the new Glyndebourne Opera House, 1994, by Michael Hopkins Partners, while theatre-in-the-round and the rediscovered thrust stage have both profoundly influenced modern theatre design.

Some of Britain's most recent theatres can stand comparison with any of their predecessors, combining brilliant functionality with sheer magic.

# Places to visit

## MUSEUMS

*The V & A Museum*, Cromwell Road, South Kensington. London SW7 2RL.
Telephone: 020 7942 2000. Website: www.vam.ac.uk
There is now no national museum in Britain dedicated to theatre. The Theatre and Performance Collections at the V & A have massive holdings, a good display space and highly expert staff. Despite the museum's distance from London's Theatreland, it has to be a natural port of call for any visitor to London with interests in any aspect of theatre. Its research collections include some thousands of drawings by theatre architects, including Frank Matcham and Bertie Crewe.

*University of Bristol Theatre Collection*, Cantocks Close, Bristol BS8 1UP.
Telephone: 0117 331 5086. Website: www.bris.ac.uk/theatrecollection/
This is a theatre collection of national importance focusing on British theatre history, with original documents, photographs and artefacts from theatres, actors, designers and more. They hold the archives of London's Old Vic and the Bristol Old Vic, as well as the late Richard Southern's mainly architectural collection and the Ray Mander and Joe Mitchenson Theatre Collection. Their online catalogue gives information for over 100,000 items.

## THEATRES

Where theatre buildings are in their designed use, the best approach is to buy a ticket and see them in action. If you want to see beyond the auditorium and public spaces, more and more theatres today hold open days or have bookable backstage tours.

Theatres that have been converted to other uses may be more difficult to get into and you are unlikely, in any case, to see them as they were meant to be seen, with box drapes, rich curtains, theatre lighting and the hubbub of theatre life. However, joining a bingo club will get you into a number of 'sleepers'.

Any tourists' guide to theatres of national importance is likely to be challenged for both its inclusions and omissions, but for those who wish to follow a theatrical itinerary the following list may be a useful starting point. Inclusion in the list does not imply that you will be able to see the interior. 'Dark' indicates that the building is at present disused. If followed by (a), access may be possible by prior arrangement.

*Note*: The current or last-known use (2011) is given where the building is not in use for some form of public entertainment. The dates given are generally those of the opening of the present building on the site. Most theatres have undergone some later alteration and in some (for example London, Adelphi and Bristol Theatre Royal) the record is so complex that even the string of dates selected for inclusion can give only an approximate indication of the phases of development visible today.

**Northern Ireland**
Belfast — Grand Opera House (1895)

**Scotland**
Aberdeen — His Majesty's (1906)
Tivoli (1872) dark
Ayr — Gaiety (1902 and 1904)
Green's Playhouse (1924) bingo
Bo'ness — Hippodrome (1912) dark
Dundee — King's (1909) pub
Edinburgh — Festival (1928 and 1994)
King's (1906)
Playhouse (1929)
Royal Lyceum (1883)
Glasgow — Britannia (c.1857–1860)
occasional performances (a)
Citizen's (1878 and 1989)
King's (1904)
Pavilion (1904)
Theatre Royal (1800 and 1895)
Inverness — Eden Court (1976)

Perth — Perth Theatre and Opera House (1900 and 1924)
Pitlochry — Festival (1981)
St Andrews — Byre Theatre (2001)

**Isle of Man**
Douglas — Gaiety (1893 and 1900)

**Wales**
Abercrave — Adelina Patti Theatre, Craig-y-Nos (1891) private, but with occasional public events
Aberystwyth — Coliseum (1905) museum
Cardiff — New (1906 and 1988)
Philharmonic Hall (1886 much altered) pub
Prince of Wales (1878 and 1920 much altered) pub
Swansea — Grand (1897)
Palace (1888) dark

*At the opera.*

## North-west England

| | |
|---|---|
| Blackpool | Grand (1894) |
| | Opera House (1939) |
| | Tower Circus (1894) |
| | Winter Gardens Pavilion (1897) conference hall |
| Burnley | Empire (1894 and 1911) dark |
| Crewe | Lyceum (1889 and 1994) |
| Lancaster | Grand (1782, 1848, 1897, etc) |
| Liverpool | Empire (1925 and 1998) |
| | Neptune (1911) |
| | Olympia (1905) occasional live use |
| | Playhouse (1898, 1911, 1968, 2001) |
| | Royal Court (1938) music venue |
| Manchester | Hulme Hippodrome (1901) dark |
| | Hulme Playhouse (1902) dark |
| | Opera House (1912) |
| | Palace (1891 and 1913) |
| | Royal Exchange (1976 and 1996) |
| | Theatre Royal (1845, etc) nightclub |
| Morecambe | Victoria Pavilion (1897) dark (a) |
| Nelson | Palace Hippodrome (1909) bingo |
| Oldham | Coliseum (1887, 1939, etc) |
| Salford | Lowry (2000) |
| | Victoria (1899) bingo |
| Stockport | Plaza (1932) |

## North-east England

| | |
|---|---|
| Billingham | Forum (1968) |
| Consett | Globe (1895 much altered) club |
| Darlington | Civic (1907) |
| Middlesbrough | Empire (1899) pub |
| Newcastle upon Tyne | Theatre Royal (1837, 1901 and 1988) |
| | Tyne Theatre and Opera House (1867) |
| Sunderland | Empire (1907) |
| Wallsend | Borough (1909) bingo |

## Yorkshire

| | |
|---|---|
| Barnsley | Theatre Royal (1898) nightclub |
| Bradford | Alhambra (1914) |
| Doncaster | Grand (1899) dark |
| Halifax | Victoria/Civic (1901) |
| Harrogate | Harrogate Theatre (1900) |
| | Royal Hall (1903) |
| Huddersfield | Lawrence Batley (converted chapel 1994) |
| Leeds | City Varieties (1865) |
| | Grand Theatre and Opera House (1878) |
| Richmond | Georgian Theatre (1788) |
| Scarborough | Stephen Joseph (interior 1996) |
| Sheffield | Crucible (1971) |
| | Lyceum (1897) |

| | |
|---|---|
| Wakefield | Theatre Royal and Opera House (1894) |
| York | Grand Opera House (1902, 1916, 1989) |
| | Theatre Royal (1765, 1835, 1880, 1902, 1967) |

## East Midlands

| | |
|---|---|
| Buxton | Opera House (1903) |
| Chatsworth | Private theatre (1830) |
| Derby | Hippodrome (1914) bingo |
| Northampton | Derngate (1983) |
| | Royal (1884) |
| Nottingham | Malt Cross (1877) bar restaurant |
| | Playhouse (1963) |
| | Theatre Royal (1865, 1897, 1978) |
| Stanford-on-Soar | Stanford Hall (1938) private theatre |

## West Midlands

| | |
|---|---|
| Birmingham | Hippodrome (1900, 1925, 2000) |
| Coventry | Belgrade (1958) |
| Newcastle-under-Lyme | New Vic (1984) |
| Stoke-on-Trent | Regent (1929 and 1999) |
| Stratford-upon-Avon | Royal Shakespeare and Swan (1879, 1932, 2010) |
| Wolverhampton | Grand (1894) |

## South Midlands

| | |
|---|---|
| Cheltenham | Everyman (1891) |
| Oxford | New (1933) |
| | Playhouse (1938) |

## East of England

| | |
|---|---|
| Bury St Edmunds | Theatre Royal (1819) |
| Cambridge | Festival (1814 and 1926) Buddhist temple |
| Colchester | Hippodrome (1905) nightclub |
| Great Yarmouth | Hippodrome (1903) |
| | Regent (1914) bingo |
| Ipswich | Wolsey (1979) |
| Norwich | Theatre Royal (1935) |
| Westcliff-on-Sea | Palace (1912) |

## South-west England

| | |
|---|---|
| Barnstaple | Queen's (as a theatre 1952, 1994) |
| Bath | Palace (1886, 1895, etc) bingo |
| | Theatre Royal, Orchard Street (1750, etc) Masonic hall |
| | Theatre Royal, Sawclose |

|             | (1805, 1863 altered)                        |
|-------------|---------------------------------------------|
| Bournemouth | Boscombe Hippodrome (1895) nightclub        |
|             | Pavilion (1929)                             |
| Bristol     | Hippodrome (1912)                           |
|             | Theatre Royal/Bristol Old Vic (1766, 1790, 1800, 1881, 1973) |
| Ilfracombe  | Landmark (1998)                             |
| Plymouth    | Theatre Royal (1982)                        |

**South-east England**

| | |
|-------------|---------------------------------------------|
| Brighton    | Hippodrome (1901) dark                      |
|             | Theatre Royal (1807, 1867, 1927)            |
| Canterbury  | Alexandra (mid nineteenth century) pub/music venue |
| Chichester  | Festival Theatre (1962)                     |
| Eastbourne  | Devonshire Park (1884 and 1903)             |
|             | Royal Hippodrome (1883)                     |
| Glyndebourne| Opera House (1994)                          |
| Horsham     | Christ's Hospital (1974)                     |
| Leatherhead | Thorndike (1969) church                     |
| Margate     | Theatre Royal (1787 and 1874)               |
| Portsmouth  | New Theatre Royal (1882 and 1900)           |
| Southampton | Mayflower (1928)                            |
| Southsea    | King's (1907)                               |
| Tunbridge Wells | Opera House (1902) pub                  |
| Watford     | Palace (1908)                               |
| Winchester  | Theatre Royal (1913 and 2002)               |
| Windsor     | Theatre Royal (1902 and 1912)               |

**London**

Adelphi (mainly 1930, parts of 1869, 1882 and 1993)
Aldwych (1905)
Ambassador's (1913)
Apollo (1901)
Apollo Victoria (1930)
Barbican (1982)
Brixton Academy (1929) music venue
Cambridge (1930)
Camden (1901) nightclub
Clapham Grand (1900) nightclub
Comedy (1881)
Coronet, Notting Hill (1898) cinema
Criterion (1874, 1884, 1992)
Dominion (1929)
Drury Lane Theatre Royal (1812, 1822, 1922)
Duchess (1929)
Duke of York's (1892)
Finsbury Park Astoria (1930) church
Fortune (1924)
Garrick (1889)
Gaumont State, Kilburn (1937)
Gielgud (1906)
Golders Green Hippodrome (1913) dark
Hackney Empire (1901 and 2004)
Haymarket Theatre Royal (1821 and 1905)
Her Majesty's (1897)
Hippodrome (1900, 1909, 2011) casino
Ivor Novello (1905)
Hoxton Hall (1863 and 1867)
London Coliseum (1904 and 2004)
London Palladium (as theatre 1910)
Lyceum (1834, 1904, 1996)
Lyric, Shaftesbury Avenue (1888)
Lyric Hammersmith (1979 recreation and 2004)
Noel Coward (1903)
Normansfield Private Theatre (1879)
Old Vic (1818, 1871, 1983)
Palace (1891)
Phoenix (1930)
Piccadilly (1929)
Playhouse (1882, 1907, 1986)
Prince Edward (1930 and 1993)
Prince of Wales (1937 and 2004)
Queen's (1908 and 1959)
Richmond Theatre (1899)
RADA Jerwood Vanbrugh (2000)
Royal Court (1888 and 2000)
Royal National Theatre (1976)
Royal Opera House (1858, 1982, 1999)
St Martin's (1916)
Savoy (1929)
Shaftesbury (1911)
Shepherd's Bush Empire (1903) music venue
Stratford East Theatre Royal (1884, 1902, 2003)
Streatham Hill Theatre (1929) bingo
Tooting Granada (1931) bingo
Tottenham Palace (1908) church
Trafalgar Studios (Whitehall) (1930, 2004)
Tricycle (1980 and 1989)
Vaudeville (1870, 1887, 1926)
Victoria Palace (1911)
Wilton's Music Hall (1859 and 1878)
Wimbledon Theatre (1910)
Wood Green Gaumont Palace (1934) church and nightclub
Woolwich Granada (1937) bingo
Wyndham's (1899)
Young Vic (1970, 2006)

# Some notable theatre architects

Any list of surviving works by British theatre architects is bound to be heavily weighted toward the late-Victorian and Edwardian boom in theatre building. The works of some of the most inventive theatre designers were devastated during the twentieth century, so that Wylson & Long, for example, are now represented here by only two substantial buildings. Frank Matcham, the most prolific of them all, unsurprisingly leads the field but, even here, the surviving theatres represent only a fraction of his lifetime output.

The selection for each architect gives preference to those where the original design has undergone relatively little subsequent alteration. The works are arranged in chronological order.

(* = now in regular live entertainment use)

**J. J. Alley**
| | |
|---|---|
| 1901 | Manchester, Hulme Hippodrome |
| 1902 | Manchester, Hulme Playhouse |

**George Coles**
| | |
|---|---|
| 1937 | London, Kilbrun Gaumont State |
| 1937 | London, Tower Hamlets Troxy |

**Bertie Crewe**
| | |
|---|---|
| 1900 | Salford, Victoria |
| *1904 | Glasgow, Pavilion |
| *1911 | London, Shaftesbury Theatre |
| 1913 | London, Golders Green Hippodrome |
| *1913 | Manchester, Palace (auditorium) |

**Robert Cromie (Emblin Walker, Jones & Cromie)**
| | |
|---|---|
| *1922 | London, Drury Lane Theatre Royal (auditorium only) |
| *1937 | London, Prince of Wales |

**Walter Emden**
| | |
|---|---|
| *1889 | London, Garrick |
| *1892 | London, Duke of York's |

**John Fairweather**
| | |
|---|---|
| 1924 | Ayr, Green's Playhouse |
| *1929 | Edinburgh, Playhouse |

**Hope & Maxwell**
| | |
|---|---|
| *1897 | Swansea, Grand |

**Cecil Masey**
| | |
|---|---|
| *1910 | London, Wimbledon Theatre (with Roy Young) |
| *1930 | London, Phoenix (with Scott & Crewe & Theodore Komisarjevsky) |

**Frank Matcham**
| | |
|---|---|
| *1891 | Cheltenham, Everyman |
| *1894 | Blackpool, Grand |

*A great variety palace of 1901 is a place of delight more than a century later. 'Slava's Snow Show' at Hackney Empire.*

| *1894 | Blackpool, Tower Circus |
| *1894 | Wakefield, Theatre Royal and Opera House |
| *1895 | Belfast, Grand Opera House |
| *1895 | London, Lyric Hammersmith (reconstructed 1979) |
| 1898 | Leeds, County Arcade (adjoining demolished Empire Palace) |
| *1899 | Blackpool, Tower Ballroom (not a theatre but a highly theatrical design) |
| *1899 | London, Richmond Theatre |
| *1900 | Douglas (Isle of Man) Gaiety |
| 1900 | London, Hippodrome (exterior) |
| *1900 | Portsmouth, New Theatre Royal (recast interior) |
| 1901 | Brighton, Hippodrome |
| *1901 | London, Hackney Empire |
| *1901 | Newcastle upon Tyne, Theatre Royal (interior) |
| *1903 | Buxton, Opera House |
| *1903 | Harrogate, Royal Hall |
| *1903 | London, Shepherd's Bush Empire |
| *1904 | Glasgow, King's |
| *1904 | London, London Coliseum |
| *1906 | Aberdeen, His Majesty's |
| 1905 | Liverpool, Olympia |
| *1907 | Southsea, King's |
| *1910 | London, London Palladium |
| *1911 | London, Victoria Palace |
| *1912 | Bristol, Hippodrome |

**W. & T. R. Milburn**

| *1907 | Sunderland, Empire |
| *1925 | Liverpool, Empire |
| *1928 | Southampton, Mayflower |
| *1929 | London, Dominion |

**C. J. Phipps**

| *1863 | Bath, Theatre Royal |
| *1880 and 1895 | Glasgow, Theatre Royal |
| *1883 | Eastbourne, Royal Hippodrome |
| *1883 | Edinburgh, Royal Lyceum |
| *1884 | Northampton, Royal |
| *1888 | London, Lyric (Shaftesbury Avenue) |
| *1894 | Wolverhampton, Grand |

| *1897 | London, Her Majesty's |

**J. T. Robinson**

| *1871 | London, Old Vic (auditorium) |
| *1874 | Margate, Theatre Royal (auditorium) |

**Ernest Runtz**

| 1899 | Middlesbrough, Empire |
| *1906 | Cardiff, New (Runtz & Ford) |

**W. G. R. Sprague**

| *1897 | Sheffield, Lyceum |
| 1898 | London, Coronet |
| *1899 | London, Wyndham's |
| 1901 | London, Camden Theatre |
| *1903 | London, Albery |
| *1905 | London, Aldwych |
| *1905 | London, Strand |
| *1906 | London, Gielgud |
| *1908 | London, Queen's |
| *1913 | London, Ambassador's |
| *1916 | London, St Martin's |

**Edward Stone**

| *1929 | London, Brixton Academy |
| *1929 | London, Piccadilly |
| *1930 | London, Whitehall (Trafalgar Studios) |
| 1930 | London, Finsbury Park Astoria |

**Thomas Verity**

| *1874 and 1884 | London, Criterion |
| *1881 | London, Comedy |

**Frank Verity**

| *1912 | Windsor, Theatre Royal (interior) |
| 1926 | London, Plaza |

**Wylson & Long**

| 1897 | Blackpool, Winter Gardens Pavilion (auditorium) |
| 1908 | London, Tottenham Palace |

# Selective bibliography

**British theatre buildings and theatre architecture**

Earl, John, and Sell, Michael (editors). *The Theatres Trust Guide to British Theatres 1750–1950*. A. & C. Black, 2000. This is a good general reference when seeking information on specific theatres. It is a descriptive, illustrated gazetteer of around 650 theatres in Britain, whether or not they are currently in theatre use. There are brief biographies of the principal architects.

Anonymous. *Theatres; a Guide to Theatre Conservation*. English Heritage note, 1995.

Barson, Susie, and others. *Scene/Unseen: London's West End Theatres*. English Heritage, 2003. Geographical coverage is the same as Kilburn (below), but the emphasis is more on the anatomy of theatres as revealed by Derek Kendall's photographs. Like Kilburn, it contains much that is relevant to theatres everywhere.

Earl, John. 'Building the halls' in Peter Bailey (editor), *Music Hall: the Business of Pleasure*. Open University Press, 1986.

Eyles, Allen. *Old Cinemas*. Shire, 2001; reprinted 2011.

Glasstone, Victor. *Victorian and Edwardian Theatres*. Thames & Hudson, 1975. Still the best, splendidly illustrated, introduction to the period.

Gray, Richard. *Cinemas in Britain*. Lund Humphries, 1996.

Kilburn, Mike. *London's Theatres*. New Holland, 2002. Although the coverage is limited to central London, the text contains many thoughtful reflections on theatre architecture and the illustrations by Alberto Arzoz are superb.

Leacroft, Richard. *Development of the English Playhouse*. Methuen, 1973.

Mackintosh, Iain, and Sell, Michael (editors). *Curtains!!! or a New Life for Old Theatres*. John Offord, 1982. A gazetteer, the forerunner of that in *The Theatres Trust Guide*, 2000. It has been overtaken by that work's more extensive coverage, but it contains a number of theatres in the Irish Republic not included in the *Guide*. The polemical introductory section also now has some historic interest in its own right.

Peter, Bruce. *Scotland's Splendid Theatres*. Polygon, 1999.

**British theatre architects**

Garlick, Görel. *To Serve the Purpose of the Drama: the Theatre Designs and Plays of Samuel Beazley 1786–1851*. Society for Theatre Research, 2003. A scholarly study of Britain's first specialist theatre architect.

Garlick, Görel. *C. J. Phipps*. A study of a leading Victorian theatre architect (in preparation).

Walker, Brian (editor). *Frank Matcham, Theatre Architect*. Blackstaff, 1980. The first detailed study of a British theatre architect, with chapters by a number of experts on theatre history.

Wilmore, David (editor). *Edwin O. Sachs: Architect, Stagehand, Engineer and Fireman*. Theatresearch, 1998.

Wilmore, David (editor). *Frank Matcham & Co*. Theatresearch 2008. A series of essays on the most prolific of all theatre architects.

*Curtain call for the star.*

# Support organisations

**Official and quasi-official bodies**
There is no official body concerned solely with theatres. The **Department for Culture, Media and Sport** has no specific unit for this purpose, and the **Arts Councils** (for England, Scotland, Wales and Northern Ireland) have shown diminishing interest in the housing of the arts.

**English Heritage (Historic Buildings and Monuments Commission)** is the official national guardian of all ancient monuments and historic buildings for England. It carries out, from time to time, detailed studies of building types, including theatres. It published a useful and practical advice note on works to historic theatres and also published (2003) a study of London's West End theatres, *Scene/Unseen*. Both are listed in the bibliography. It is worth noting that most theatres of any architectural quality are now protected listed buildings and information on them can be obtained in the statutory lists, most of which are now available online (*see* National Monuments Record). *English Heritage, 1 Waterhouse Square, 138-142 Holborn, London EC1N 2ST. Telephone: 020 7973 3000. Website: www.english-heritage.org.uk*

The former Royal Commission on Historical Monuments for England (RCHME), established in 1908, was the body responsible for recording ancient and historical monuments throughout the country and publishing its findings. It is now absorbed into English Heritage along with its public archive, the **National Monuments Record**, founded in 1941. The NMR is a recording body and a repository for records of historic buildings, monuments and sites. Amongst its millions of photographs and drawings are many of theatres, including a large number of negatives and prints made by the firm of Bedford Lemere, many of them before the First World War. The NMR also holds the records of the **Survey of London**. It gives online access to the statutory lists for England and, through its 'Images of England' project, to a growing archive of recent photographs of listed buildings. *National Monuments Record Centre, Great Western Village, Kemble Drive, Swindon SN2 2GZ. Telephone: 01793 414600. Website: www.english-heritage.org.uk*

**Cadw** fulfils a closely similar role to English Heritage in Wales. *Cadw, Plas Carew, Unit 5/7 Cefn Coed, Parc Nantgarw, Cardiff CF15 7QQ. Telephone: 01443 336000. Website: www.cadw.wales.gov.uk*

The **Royal Commission on the Ancient and Historical Monuments of Wales (RCAHMW)** remains independent of Cadw. A searchable database is available online. *RCAHMW, Plas Crug, Aberystwyth, Ceredigion SY23 1NJ. Telephone: 01970 621200. Website: www.rcahmw.gov.uk*

**Historic Scotland** fulfils a closely similar role to English Heritage in Scotland. *Historic Scotland, Longmore House, Salisbury Place, Edinburgh EH9 1SH. Telephone: 0131 668 8600. Website: www.historic-scotland.gov.uk*

The **Royal Commission on the Ancient and Historical Monuments of Scotland (RCAHMS)** remains independent of Historic Scotland. It was founded in 1908 to record monuments throughout Scotland. Photographic and drawn surveys have been carried out on theatres all over Scotland, mostly in Glasgow and Edinburgh but also in Dumfries, Inverness and Aberdeen. Records can be queried online and the number of images available is growing. Historic Scotland's listed building information and RCAHMS data are now available jointly through the Pastmap database on the RCAHMS website. *RCAHMS, John Sinclair House, 16 Bernard Terrace, Edinburgh EH8 9NX. Telephone: 0131 662 1456. Website: www.rcahms.gov.uk*

**Statutory bodies**
There is only one relevant statutory body: **The Theatres Trust.**
The Trust was created by Parliament in 1976 to promote the better protection of theatres for the benefit of the nation. It has the right to be consulted by (not merely to offer comments to) all planning authorities on applications that affect land on which there is a theatre. It is concerned with all theatre buildings, old or new, listed or unlisted, in use as theatres, in other uses or disused. Its major concern is with the protection of theatres as a cultural resource. Its quarterly journal, *Theatres Magazine*, is a rich source of topical and historical information. The Trust maintains and constantly updates a detailed database of some thousands of theatres, extant and demolished, in all parts of Britain. The database is being made progressively available online. *The Theatres Trust, 22 Charing Cross Road, London WC2H 0QL. Telephone: 020 7836 8591.*
*Website: www.theatrestrust.org.uk*

**National preservation societies**

The national organisations listed below have no official status but they are recognised by the responsible government departments and by English Heritage as authoritative voices for the periods their names suggest. All listed building demolition applications are referred to them and they have the opportunity to offer informed comments and to exert pressure for refusal when they see fit. They also keep careful watch on all other matters affecting their interest. In most instances, when considering a theatre case, they consult with The Theatres Trust (but are not required to do so).

Society for the Protection of Ancient Buildings
   37 Spital Square, London E1 6DY. Telephone: 020 7377 1644. Website: www.spab.org.uk

Ancient Monuments Society
   St Ann's Vestry Hall, 2 Church Entry, London EC4V 5HB.
   Telephone: 020 7236 3934. Website: www.ancientmonumentssociety.org.uk

The Georgian Group
   6 Fitzroy Square, London W1T 5DX. Telephone: 020 7529 8920.
   Telephone: 087 1750 2936. Website: www.georgiangroup.org.uk

The Victorian Society
   1 Priory Gardens, Bedford Park, London W4 1TT.
   Telephone: 020 8994 1019. Website: www.victorian-society.org.uk

The Twentieth Century Society
   70 Cowcross Street, London EC1M 6EJ. Telephone: 020 7250 3857. Website: www.c20society.org.uk

**Special interest groups**

Although not included in any arrangements for the reference of applications, the following pursue their interests in a similar way to national preservation societies and may, in some cases, be consulted informally by national and local authorities.

SAVE Britain's Heritage

A campaigning and publishing group with an impressive record for focusing public interest on classes of threatened buildings.

*Goodbye to Scarborough's Royal Opera House, demolished 2004.*

*SAVE Britain's Heritage, 70 Cowcross Street, London EC1M 6EJ. Telephone: 020 7253 3500. Website: www.savebritainsheritage.org*

Save Britain's Theatres
Campaigning body (in course of formation 2011).

Cinema Theatre Association
The Association was founded in 1967 to promote serious interest in all aspects of cinema buildings. Its periodical publication *Picture House* contains authoritative articles on cinemas (many of which were also theatres) with lavish illustrations.
*The Cinema Theatre Association, 128 Gloucester Terrace, London W2 6HP. Website: www.cinema-theatre.org.uk*

Frank Matcham Society
The Society is not solely concerned with this architect but with the appreciation of fine theatres everywhere. Members receive a regular illustrated newsletter containing information about individual theatres.
*Ann Kendal, Secretary, 9 Ruskin Court, Bradford Road, Wakefield WF1 2BN. Telephone: 01924 378349. Website: www.frankmatchamsociety.org.uk*

British Music Hall Society
The society has an active research group. Its periodical publication *The Callboy* frequently contains items on buildings.
*Howard Lee, Secretary, Thurston Lodge, Thurston Park, Whitstable, Kent CT5 1RE. Telephone: 01227 275959. Website: www.music-hall-society.com*

## Sources of information
In addition to the organisations listed above, the following will be found helpful at various levels in providing information about theatres and like buildings.

Theatre and Performance Collections, V & A Museum. See Places to Visit, page 53.
A well-informed staff deal with all kinds of research and general enquiries.

Ray Mander and Joe Mitchenson Theatre Collection
Essentially a research collection and a source of illustrations. Mander and Mitchenson published many books, including two dedicated to London theatres and lost London theatres. This collection is now based at the University of Bristol Theatre Collection. See Places to Visit, page 53.

Society for Theatre Research
Although the society is not a statutory or campaigning body, its scholarly journal, *Theatre Notebook*, often contains interesting material on theatre buildings.
*The Society for Theatre Research, c/o The Theatre Museum, 1E Tavistock Street, London WC2E 7PR. Website: www.str.org.uk*

University of Bristol Theatre Collection
See Places to visit (page 53).

The following websites also contain information on theatre and music hall buildings – more than may be evident from their titles:

| | |
|---|---|
| Carthalia Theatre Postcards | www.andreas-praefcke.de/carthalia/index |
| John Culme's Footlight Notes | http://footlightnotes.tripod.com |
| Arthur Lloyd | www.arthurlloyd.co.uk |
| Backstage | www.backstage.ac.uk |

# Index

*The index embraces the text and the picture captions but does not include the appendices.*
*Figures in italics refer to illustrations or their captions.*